Alma the Younger

written by Tiffany Thomas
illustrated by Nikki Casassa

CFI • An imprint of Cedar Fort, Inc. • Springville, Utah

HARD WORDS:
younger, angel, teach, listen

PARENT TIP: Give frequent praise, especially when they keep working on a difficult word.

This is Alma
the Younger.
He is the
son of Alma.

These are the four
sons of King Mosiah.

They are all friends.

The five boys are
mean and bad.

An angel comes to
tell them to stop.

Alma the Younger
falls asleep.
Alma says a prayer.

His son has a dream
about God and repents.

Alma the Younger wakes up.
Now he is good.

The sons of Mosiah are good now, too

They teach people how to be good.

Many people listen and are now good.

The end.

This is not an official publication of The Church of Jesus Christ of Latter-day Saints. The opinions and views expressed herein belong solely to the author and do not necessarily represent the opinions or views of Cedar Fort, Inc. Permission for the use of sources, graphics, and photos is also solely the responsibility of the author.

ISBN 13: 978-1-4621-4337-5

Published by CFI, an imprint of Cedar Fort, Inc. • 2373 W. 700 S., Suite 100, Springville, UT 84663
Distributed by Cedar Fort, Inc., www.cedarfort.com

Cover design and interior layout design by Shawnda T. Craig
Cover design © 2022 Cedar Fort, Inc.
Printed in China • Printed on acid-free paper
10 9 8 7 6 5 4 3 2 1